The Wisdom of the Jewish Mystics

The Wisdom of
the Jewish Mystics

Translated by

Alan Unterman

For Nechama

Axios Press
P.O. Box 118
Mount Jackson, VA 22842
888.542.9467   info@axiospress.com

Library of Congress Cataloging-in-Publication Data

The wisdom of the Jewish mystics / translated by Alan Unterman.
    p. cm.
    Reprint. Originally published: London : Sheldon Press, 1976.
    Includes bibliographical references and index.
    ISBN 978-1-60419-013-7 (alk. paper)
    1.Cabala—Translations into English. 2. Hasidism. I. Unterman, Alan.

BM525.A2W57 2009
296.1'6--dc22

                                        2009013769

Contents

Part 1

The Wisdom of
the Jewish Mystics

T**HE JEWISH MYSTICAL** tradition of theosophical teaching and practice, which aims at direct
encounter between man's soul and God, has
its roots deep in the Jewish past yet lives on within the
religious milieu of the Jewish present. In different parts
of the globe, from Montreal or Brooklyn in the West
to Jerusalem, B'nai Braq or Safed in the East, the teachings of the Jewish mystics throughout the ages are studied, and the mystic path which they have laid out with
great care and love is assiduously followed. To the out-
sider, the contemporary Jewish mystic may seem quite
ordinary; one could pass him in a typical Jerusalem
side street without a second glance. Yet he possesses

an inner world of infinite richness and color. He shuffles along the road dressed in dark clothes, turns into a dimly lit synagogue whose interior is drab and seems distinguished only by the chaotic arrangement of its tables and benches, and sits down in front of a rather shabby book. This book may be any one of dozens of mystical texts, most probably it is one of the volumes of the Zohar, the *Book of Splendour*, written in a curious Aramaic and regarded as the Bible of Jewish mysticism. Before opening the book he sits for a moment with his eyes closed, and meditates, utters a prayer, or mumbles over and over the words: "Open my eyes so that I may perceive the wonders of Your teaching." He is about to enter a world very different from the world he sees about him; a world of symbols and images before which the hard empirical reality of his environment melts into insubstantial shadows. As he opens the volume of the Zohar and chants its strange cadences a glazed look comes into his eyes, his inner world begins to open up to the power of the Jewish theosophical symbols. His soul has taken flight to dimensions which the mystics simply refer to as "the upper worlds," with flushed face he unifies the upper and lower worlds within himself. Unfortunately we cannot follow him into the symbolic world of the Zohar, for he has embarked on a journey into the infinity of the Godhead, exploring the divine structures and dimensions which lie under the surface of the everyday reality which represents the limits of the world that we know.

The sheer complexity of the mystical symbolism of Jewish theosophy excludes the merely curious collector of exotica from anything more than a glimpse into what must seem like a confusion of sound and light, of near mythological fancy and images. Yet even he can perceive that something, he knows not what, is being said by these mystical descriptions and allusions. For the mystic himself the symbolism provides a framework, both beautiful and profound, within which his own experience finds its full expression. As the general name for the Jewish mystical tradition, Kabbalah (literally "Received Tradition"), itself indicates, the mystic receives the inner meaning of the theosophical tradition from a master or teacher, who provides the key to a correct understanding of the texts. Book knowledge alone may provide an academic veneer but gives no real insight. The following is a description of his encounter with his teacher from the pen of one of the outstanding mystics of the last generation, R. Judah L. Ashlag:

> On the 12th of the Hebrew month Marheshvan, on a Friday morning, a certain man came to see me. It was apparent to me that he was a great and wonderful sage in the wisdom of the Kabbalah . . . and immediately he started speaking I felt that the wisdom of God was within him. . . . He promised to teach me the True Wisdom in all its completeness, and I studied with him for three months, every night after midnight, in his house. Most of

the study was about how to live a holy and pure life, but each time I was insistent that he reveal to me some secret of the kabbalistic wisdom. He began to teach me some general outlines, but he would never actually teach me anything completely. Naturally I had a great longing to know something substantial, until eventually after I grew very insistent he taught me a kabbalistic secret in its completeness. My joy was without bounds. And from that time my ego began to swell, and the more sense of self I acquired the more my holy master removed himself from me, and at the time I did not even realize what was happening. Things went on like this for three months and at the end of that period I could never find my master at his house. I sought him but I could not find him. Then I realized that he was really distancing himself from me, and I was very distressed and started to improve my ways. On the 9th of the Hebrew month Nisan, in the morning, I found him . . . and was able to reestablish my relationship to him as before, and he revealed to me a great mystical secret . . . which made me rejoice. But I noticed that he was becoming very weak, and so I stayed with him in his house. The very next day he died. . . . My pain was beyond expression. . . . I was left naked and deprived of everything, and I even forgot what I had learned from him because of my grief. From then on I lifted up my eyes with immeasurable longing and did not rest . . . until I found favor with my Maker . . . and he opened my heart to the higher wisdom . . . and I also remembered the secrets which I had received from my master. . . . My master had considerable business interests, and was well known as an honest merchant . . . but to this day nobody knows of his kabbalistic wisdom, and he refused me permission to reveal his name.

One of the prerequisites of the study of Kabbalah is the perfecting of the personality, removing the pride and selfishness, the "me" and "mine," which inflate the ego and block one's ability to receive the "True Wisdom." This is done, in part, by the Jewish religion itself which, through its rituals and responsibilities, disciplines a man and refines his animal nature. But more than this is needed, and it was once accepted practice not to initiate someone into the mystical tradition unless he was married, and therefore of a more stable libido, of mature years, and knowledgeable in the study of Jewish religious texts. Nowadays these conditions have generally been waived, which makes the requirement of self-perfection all the more important. There are two sides to the receiving of kabbalistic wisdom. On one side is the master, whom one must find or who will find one, and on the other is the disciple who must make himself a vessel capable of receiving.

A Hasidic master of the eighteenth century, R. Mendel of Premyslan, explained that real secrets or mysteries are things which cannot be expressed by a man to his fellow; they have to be experienced at first hand. Thus it is impossible truly to describe a particular taste to someone who has never eaten the dish in question. What is commonly thought of as esoteric or mysterious in Judaism is written down and there for everyone to read. If someone is a fool and does not understand, then every text is an esoteric one. What makes the Kabbalah a mystery is that its understanding depends on the state of man's inner self, his soul. If he has reached the point of inward cleaving to God then he will be able to understand what he is taught from his own spiritual experience, from within, as it were.

The kabbalistic tradition, the hidden teaching (*nistar*), exists side-by-side with the non-esoteric everyday religion of Judaism (*nigleh*). The esoteric teaching is thought of as a deeper dimension of the nonesoteric religion, but it is perfectly possible to be a full Jew, living out a life imbued, with the Jewish spirit, without having any insight into Kabbalah at all. Nevertheless the kabbalist cannot help thinking of the Jew who remains on the purely non-esoteric or exoteric level as someone whose life is religiously impoverished and one-dimensional. The Zohar even refers to those who take everyday Judaism as the totality of Judaism or as its deepest layer, in very negative terms, and calls them outright fools. Perhaps today's kabbalist would prefer to express it by saying that such an attitude is not conducive to a fulfilled religious life.

Not only is it true that one does not have to be a kabbalist to be a devout Jew, it is also true that one does not have to be a mystic to be a kabbalist. The way of the Kabbalah, the study and practices associated with it, are followed by people who are in no sense genuine mystics. They are mystics by proxy, as it were, who have no experiential understanding of the symbolic structures, do not learn at the feet of a master, nor have they reached an inner level of holiness and moral purity. To call them kabbalists is perhaps a little far-fetched, but they are certainly kabbalistic fellow travelers and they make up the vast bulk of those who study and pray in the kabbalistic way. For some, the symbols, though barely grasped, convey a suggestiveness and majesty which reverberates within. For others the texts of Kabbalah, particularly the Zohar, are so holy that merely chanting them aloud is considered a meritorious act, and generates a sincere feeling of awe and of the divine presence. There is no doubt that these fellow travelers have contributed, almost as much as card-carrying mystics, to the preservation of the kabbalistic teaching down the ages.

The kabbalistic tradition is made up of a number of different components, many of which we would not associate with mysticism as understood in the West. It is difficult, therefore, to locate the origins of mysticism as a clearly identifiable phenomenon in the long history of Jewish religious experience. The encounter between Israel and God, as depicted, for instance, in the revelation at Sinai, may or may not be understood as a mystical encounter depending on how widely we wish to use the term "mysticism." For the Kabbalah the revelation at Sinai is an encounter full of kabbalistic significance, but this is no guide since everything in the Bible is understood by the Kabbalah as an expression of its own esotericism.

The same sort of ambiguity surrounds the records of the prophetic visions of the heavenly world. The prophet Isaiah sees the LORD sitting on the divine throne and hears the Seraphim call out to one another, "Holy, holy, holy is the LORD of Hosts." The prophet Ezekiel records an extensive vision of the heavenly world of angelic creatures and forms surrounding the divine throne. Whether we are to understand these visions as mystic/prophetic in nature depends, once again, on our approach to the mystical element in Judaism. What is clear is that the later kabbalistic tradition, while taking these biblical accounts as mystical patterns, is much closer to mysticism as generally understood in Christianity, Sufism, or the religions of the East than any of the biblical phenomena.

We first come across Jewish mysticism in a recognizable form in the Mishnaic/Talmudic period beginning perhaps a century or so before the Christian era and extending past the editing of the Babylonian Talmud in the sixth century. Mysticism in Jewish texts of this period (i.e., the Mishnah, Talmud, Tosefta, and Midrash) is depicted not merely as a sectarian phenomenon, though clearly there were many sectarian mystical groups on the fringes of rabbinic Judaism, but as the province of rabbis and sages who were the pillars of the Talmudic establishment. These same rabbis played a major role in the development of the nonmystical teachings of rabbinic Judaism. A case in point is R. Akiva (c. 50–135) about whose mystical life we know very little except that he was a leading mystic of the time. R. Akiva's influence on the halakhic, or legal, side of Judaism was without parallel in the second century as is brought out in the Talmudic tale of Moses coming back to sit at R. Akiva's feet and not understanding his lectures.

The mysticism of the Mishnaic and Talmudic periods turned around two central pivots: (a) Speculation about the generation of the universe in the account of the Creation, and therefore about the relationship between God and His world, and more importantly (b) contemplative mysticism surrounding the vision of the divine chariot, or throne, based on the description in the Book of Ezekiel. This latter was essentially an esoteric doctrine which the Mishnah recommends should be taught only to a single student at a time, and on the condition that he already understands the material involved, while the former concerning the origins of the universe were open to the uninitiated again provided that they received personal tuition from the master.

The path of the Jewish mystic towards his goal of a vision of the divine chariot took him through various levels or stages, each of which was fraught with danger. Much of the surviving literature is concerned with providing the adept with techniques of passage from level to level, and not everyone who undertook the mystical journey into Paradise returned safe and sound. The Talmudic tale of the four sages who entered Paradise served as a warning for would-be mystics, for only one sage, R. Akiva, emerged unscathed. Yet for all the otherworldliness of these visionary flights the Jewish mystic remained rooted in the earthiness of everyday reality. The sage/mystic of this period was no monastic; he did not preach asceticism, nor did he escape into the desert as did sectarian groups like those of the Qumran community. He advocated an ideal of marriage, family life, and communal responsibility coupled with his contemplative mysticism. The more rooted and stable a man was the less chance that his visions would unbalance him for life in the world, and prevent him from fulfilling himself as a total human being.

This duality of otherworldliness and earthiness so characteristic of the sage/mystic of Talmudic times continued as a basic structure of Jewish mysticism from henceforth. In each age the emphasis differed, fluctuating from a near asceticism to a mystical consecration of the everyday, but the basic duality was only broken at the risk of mystical sectarianism. The tensions within the elements of this duality may be seen as one of the creative forces which allowed the Jewish mystical tradition to continually renew itself.

In the post-Talmudic period the contemplative mysticism of the vision of the divine chariot developed in new directions both among the Jews of Germany and among those of the Iberian Peninsula. Whereas the former took on a fervently pious bent under the leadership of R. Judah the Pietist, whose literary testimony is contained in the work *Sefer Hasidim*, the latter deepened the theosophical component of the Kabbalah and developed a rich symbolic language in which to express it. It was amongst circles of Spanish mystics that the various parts of the Zohar were finally redacted in the late thirteenth century, and it is to them that later Kabbalah owes its thought forms and direction. The Zohar was soon accepted as a standard kabbalistic work, and the power of its imagery and symbols made it a textbook for all future mystical undercurrents in Judaism. It succeeded in bringing together many of the different mystical strands within the Judaism of the period, and represented itself as the mystical teachings first formulated by R. Simeon bar Yohai and his school in second-century Palestine. The kabbalists themselves were aware that there were too many anachronisms to allow all the teachings of the Zohar to be actually those of the second or third centuries, but they were unconcerned with historical detail. R. Simeon bar Yohai was the archetypal mystic and by affirming the Zoharic theosophy to be a product of his school they were emphasizing the continuity of the mystical tradition.

The main motif of the mysticism of the Zohar was the theosophical pattern of divine structures underlying both the everyday world and the complexity of Jewish rituals and practices. Through these structures the mystic was able to unify his own experience and the ideas and values of his tradition into a single whole. Man was seen as a microcosm, paralleling within himself the workings of God within the cosmos, and his inner and outer worlds were reflections of each other. The self-explorations of the kabbalist in mystical experience were at the same time theosophical explorations of the divinely controlled reality.

In the period following the expulsion of the Jews from Spain in the late fifteenth century the teachings of the Spanish kabbalists spread throughout North Africa and the Levant. The upheaval and the shock of exile caused by the expulsion brought about a new stirring of the Jewish mystical consciousness which culminated in the teachings of a circle of mystics in Safed, Northern Palestine, in the second half of the sixteenth century. Here a group of exiles gathered themselves around a number of key mystical figures, such as R. Moses Cordovero and R. Isaac Luria, who produced a series of new and profound developments of the kabbalistic theosophy. The mystical innovator of the Safed circle was R. Isaac Luria, known as the holy Ari, and in the course of a short teaching ministry he gave the Zoharic symbols an interpretation which allowed them to encompass the experience of exile, upheaval, suffering, and redemption by placing these elements in the Godhead itself. The Lurianic Kabbalah taught a mystical messianism which captured the religious imagination both of his immediate followers and later of a much wider audience through the books of the master's teachings which were published.

Less than a century after the death of R. Isaac Luria the powerful messianic element within his theosophy gave rise to a movement which swept through the Jewish world, eventually leaving a trail of havoc and mystical heresy amongst the Jewish communities of Europe and the East. This movement centered around the strange figure of Shabbetai Zevi (1626–1676), who declared himself the Messiah and won the support of large sections of Jewry including some of the most eminent rabbis of the time. When Shabbetai Zevi was forced by the Turkish authorities to renounce Judaism in favor of Islam, most of his erstwhile supporters deserted him. Those that remained were able to interpret the actions of their "Messiah" in terms of the Shabbetian Kabbalah which taught that it was necessary for the Messiah to descend into the depths in order to redeem the elements of holiness which were trapped there. This doctrine was eventually to lead to strong currents of antinomianism, the belief that the traditional law is not binding on Jews, both within this new breakaway sectarian group, and within the

Frankist movement led by Jacob Frank (1726–1791) which left Judaism altogether when it nominally converted to Catholicism.

Following the messianic debacle, and the consequent antinomianism, there was a shying away from kabbalistic speculation and a conscious attempt by the mystics themselves to defuse the influence of Lurianic theosophy on the minds of the masses. This rejection of the messianic intensity brought forth a new awareness of the rootedness of the kabbalistic symbolism in the everyday life of the individual and the community. In the mid-eighteenth century Jewish mysticism was given a new direction by Israel Baal Shem Tov (1700–1760), commonly called the Besht, who emphasized the psychological dimension of the Kabbalah and was thus able to reconstitute the Lurianic system from the midst of the Shabbetian trauma, and its Frankist aftermath. The Besht acted as a catalyst bringing together a galaxy of innovative mystics who constituted the nexus of the Hasidic movement which was founded after his death. Around the Besht and the Hasidic masters who succeeded him a whole series of stories and legends were woven, and to this day they are part of the living tradition of Hasidic lore. From this vast literature we can gain an insight into the lives and teachings of these mystics which stands in stark contrast to the anonymity of the mystics of the Middle Ages.

One of the revolutionary elements which the Besht introduced into the basically Lurianic framework of the Kabbalah was the relevance of the mystical symbol to everyday religion. In this way he was able to relate as a teacher and guide both to the intellectual elite and to the unlettered Jewish peasant. Though a number of his followers were greater scholars, and even greater mystics, than the Besht, he was able to show them the existential significance of the symbols of the classical Kabbalah. The method he used was often that of the story or parable which carried with it the immediacy of the concrete as well as serving as a vehicle for some underlying kabbalistic image. The later Hasidic movement used the story form of teaching as one of its prime instruments of instruction, thereby preserving the basic existential dimension which the Besht had introduced.

The duality within Jewish mysticism between the otherworldliness of the mystic consciousness and the rootedness of the mystic in the everyday is apparent in Hasidic mysticism, but with a noticeable difference. For whereas previously the duality was maintained through an uneasy tension, the Hasidic mystic goes a considerable way in resolving this tension. The Besht taught his followers to see the divine within the ordinary, to see the everyday experience as clothing the experience of the mystic. It was this teaching which roused the opponents of Hasidism to declare holy war against the fledgling mystical sect and to brand it as pantheistic. Foremost among these opponents were two of the leading kabbalists in East Europe outside the

Hasidic camp, Elijah the Gaon of Vilna (1720–1797) and his pupil R. Haim of Volozhin (1749–1829), whose approach to Kabbalah was more along the traditional lines of the Zohar and the Ari. The controversies over whether or not Hasidic teaching was heretical were presumably initiated by the memories of the Shabbatian and Frankist movements, but they continued long after these memories had died.

The Baal Shem Tov was succeeded by R. Dov Baer, the Maggid of Mezherich, who took over the leadership of the movement and gathered around himself a circle of disciples whom he personally instructed in the new way of Hasidic mysticism. R. Dov Baer gave the insights of the Besht greater theoretical foundation, and provided an aura of intellectual respectability to Hasidism. However, it was left to one of his pupils, R. Schneur Zalman of Liadi, to formulate the first systematic theosophy of Hasidism in which the existential dimension was included side by side with kabbalistic speculation. Not all of the pupils of the Maggid agreed with this new intellectualism which they felt the Besht had been trying to eradicate from Jewish mysticism, and in their teachings we find a repeated emphasis on spontaneity and a rootedness in the concrete as the essence of the Hasidic path. One of the opponents of R. Schneur Zalman was R. Abraham of Kalisk who represents extreme enthusiastic and emotive mysticism. The followers of R. Abraham used to turn somersaults during prayer, and their strange antics were something of an embarrassment to those Hasidic leaders who were trying to make Hasidism respectable and acceptable to the non-Hasidic rabbinical leadership. Other Hasidic masters, such as R. Levi Isaac, R. Zusya or R. Shmelke, occupied a position in between the intellectualism of R. Schneur Zalman and the emotivism of R. Abraham, yet each one of the disciples created a particular version of the Hasidic path all his own. This was one of the main reasons why on the death of the Maggid, the movement split up into many sub-movements each with its own spiritual guide and its own "way."

Outside the sphere of influence of the Maggid there were other Hasidic masters who had either studied at the feet of the Besht himself or had come to his teachings in a more indirect fashion. Foremost among these latter was R. Nahman of Bratslav, the great-grandson of the Besht, who developed a unique form of Hasidic Kabbalah and who used the medium of the allegorized fairy story as a means of teaching his theosophical ideas. Though R. Nahman died in 1811 his followers still treat him as their spiritual guide, and are referred to as "Dead Hasidim" because they appointed no successors to R. Nahman.

The mystical element has died out amongst most contemporary Hasidic groups, and is kept alive only amongst Habad Hasidim who follow the path mapped out by R. Shneur Zalman of Liadi and amongst the Bratslav Hasidim who perpetuate the teachings of R.

Nahman. Nevertheless the original Hasidic mystical teachings have continued to influence the individual creative mystics of the modern age. Outstanding among the latter is R. Abraham Isaac Kook (1865–1935), who served as Chief Rabbi of Palestine and whose ideas on Jewish mysticism are slowly making their way into the Jewish religious consciousness.

The mystical tradition of Judaism is not a static one. Creative mystics have enhanced it and deepened it in each generation, and have poured the insight gained by their own mystical experience into the total framework. It is customary to describe firsthand mystical experience, which comes to the mystic from the reaches of the divine, as a revelation brought by Elijah the prophet who still acts as God's messenger to mankind. The tradition is naturally rather conservative, and it takes some time before it absorbs and accepts developments. However, as can be seen from the case of the innovations introduced into kabbalistic theosophy by R. Isaac Luria, in Safed in the second half of the sixteenth century, the tradition is open ended. All kabbalists agree that the doctrines of R. Isaac Luria are not mentioned explicitly in the pre-Lurianic writings, yet all kabbalistic teaching in the modern period is based on the Lurianic system. Indeed when a kabbalist today speaks of Kabbalah as such he means Lurianic Kabbalah.

Although the images which the Kabbalah uses are very concrete and totally anthropomorphic, and may sometimes shock the sensibilities of the unwary, they are not to be taken as anything but symbolic forms conveying understanding beyond the standard conceptual levels of logical thought. The overriding emphasis within Judaism on the indivisible unity of God underlies the whole kabbalistic theosophy and indeed it is this which allows the mystic so much freedom for symbolic description. It cannot be denied that nonkabbalists have misinterpreted the variety of the symbolic language, and the richness of its forms, finding it to be teaching a threefold or tenfold nature of the divine. But no kabbalist himself, however distinct his imagery may seem, ever misunderstood the symbol for the unitary reality behind it. Indeed it was the obvious danger of misunderstanding, of the unification of symbol and reality and the resultant heresies, which kept the Kabbalah at the level of the esoteric. We find warnings in quite early sources against the public teaching of the mystical tradition and even against the private teaching of it to those who are unable to assimilate its symbolic nature. It was the danger of misunderstanding which helped to keep the kabbalistic tradition an oral tradition, and the opposition to writing down and publishing mystical teachings exists into the present day.

From what has been said above it will be realized that it would be difficult to sketch out the symbolic theosophy of the Kabbalah in comprehensible yet unambiguous terms. It is possible to restate various kabbalistic doctrines but the reader is then entitled to ask what such doctrines in fact mean, or what relevance they could possibly have to anyone. Clearly to the kabbalists themselves the way a doctrine is expressed, the symbols used in expressing it, is not something casual or irrelevant. Indeed we sometimes find wide-ranging arguments among the kabbalists themselves about the correct formulation and interpretation of certain doctrines.

Just as the restatement of poetry in prose form is at best a gross falsification, so the restatement of kabbalistic doctrines in clinical English gives a false impression of the nature of these teachings. Kabbalah has to be studied in a way suitable to a mystical theosophy, it cannot be presented either as a system of propositional truths, or as straight theology. The knowledge which theosophy conveys is an inner knowledge; it is bound up with the way it is acquired and with the development of the man himself as he acquires it. There is a strong experiential dimension to the understanding of a kabbalistic image which cannot be conveyed by the bland analysis of the image itself.

What can be conveyed is what we might call the human face of the Kabbalah, namely the thoughts and insights of the mystics about the everyday world and the way in which they lived. To find this human side of their teachings we have to leave aside the vast bulk of the kabbalistic literature, which is intended for the initiate, and to pick out the more mundane aspects which were recorded by their pupils either as factual reports or as more fanciful legends. The Talmud itself recognized the worth of this kind of material when it laid down the principle that even the small talk of a sage is worthy of close study.

Very little data is available about the life of the Jewish mystics; what there is has to be culled from autobiographical fragments or from within their theosophical teachings. One of the reasons for this is presumably that given the doctrine of man the microcosm everything is projected outwards, so that instead of talking about his life or the psychic dimensions of his soul, the mystic is always talking about the structure of the cosmos. His own inner experience is already a theosophy.

Many of the mystics of the Talmudic period and the Middle Ages seem to have lived overtly ordinary lives, occasionally given to the life of the recluse but most commonly taking a leadership role within the community. A few were semianarchic figures whose mysticism seems to have generated a sort of bohemianism, which found its outlet in Messianic fervor. One such character was the peripatetic Spanish mystic Abraham Abulafia (thirteenth century) whose prophetic Kabbalah roused considerable interest in his own day. His messianic pretensions caused considerable upheaval amongst the Jewish communities of Europe and drew forth the condemnation of the official rabbinate. Perhaps for this reason few of his writings have survived into modern times, though his influence was felt in kabbalistic circles for several centuries after his death.

Anarchic tendencies were more frequent in the mystical heresies of a messianic nature produced under Lurianic influence. As we have seen, the movement which surrounded the mystical Messiah Shabbetai Zevi in the seventeenth century, and that surrounding Jacob Frank in the eighteenth, both passed the bounds of orthodox Jewish mysticism into antinomian heresy.

Despite these powerful upsurges of anarchy within the Jewish mystical tradition, what typified mainstream kabbalists was their strict adherence to Jewish orthodoxy and orthodox practice. The foremost example of the harmonious interrelationship between mystical ecstasy and religious conformism is that of Rabbi Joseph Karo. Though he was a member of the inner circle of mystics in Safed in the sixteenth century, he is best known as the author of three major works devoted entirely to Jewish law, and one of the foremost contributors to its codification. His skill in legal analysis and Talmudic dialectics did not interfere with his possession of a heavenly mentor who revealed mystical secrets to him. The following is a contemporary description of R. Joseph Karo's spirit possession:

> We agreed together with the saint (R. Joseph Karo) . . . to spend the evening before Pentecost awake. . . . While we were beginning to study . . . a voice was heard speaking from

> the mouth of the saint, a loud voice with
> clearly accentuated sounds. All those round
> about heard the voice but they did not under-
> stand what was happening. . . . The voice grew
> louder and we all fell on our faces and no one
> had the courage to lift up his eyes to see what
> was happening because of the great fear we all
> felt. . . . The speech was addressed to us and
> began "My friends . . ."

Our understanding of the inner life of the Jewish
mystics changes when we come to the mystical revival
of the modern period beginning with the Hasidic
movement in Eastern Europe in the later eighteenth
century. The early leaders of the movement were all
kabbalists and left behind them, not merely some of
the most profound interpretations of the Jewish theosophical tradition, but also a wide-ranging record of
their experience. The impetus for the movement came
from a desire to redirect the Jewish masses back towards
a life of religious intensity. This had to be achieved in
the face of mechanization of the religious life and lip
service on the one hand, and a highly abstruse intellectualism prevalent amongst East European rabbis on
the other. The kabbalistic symbols and images had to
be changed into terms that were comprehensible, not
merely to the inner circle of the mystical elite, but to
the Jewish artisan and petty trader as well.

All the powerful images of the Lurianic Kabbalah
find their expression in Hasidic mysticism, but each of

the Hasidic mystics adds a new dimension of interpretation to these images which bring them down to earth, as it were. The Kabbalah which Hasidism teaches is a mysticism of the immanence or presence of God, while classical Kabbalah is a theosophy of his transcendence. This emphasis on immanence brings out a tendency, inherent in Kabbalah, towards panentheism in which the whole world is conceived of as structured out of, and contained within, God Himself. Reality is the clothing of the Godhead. Behind the solidity of the inorganic world and the living, breathing, organic world is the Godhead itself towards whom the mystic breaks through by penetrating the everyday thought forms and perceptions which only tell us about the clothing, not about that which is clothed. This identification of the world with God, albeit in the sense that it is a masking of the divine, developed a sense of the holiness of the profane amongst Hasidism and greatly disturbed some of their opponents.

The Hasidic mystics, as indeed some of their kabbalistic predecessors, sought out the world of nature, the forest, the grassy field, or the mountain, as places for meditation and contemplation. They taught the Jewish masses of Poland and the Ukraine how to serve God through the everyday, the ordinary, on the premise that God is in the mundane environment just as he is in the synagogue or house of study. They used the images and objects of everyday life to convey their message, and the story form as a means of expression for profound kabbalistic symbols. Song and dance became techniques for elevating the soul to God, and alcohol and tobacco were sanctified and given a mystical rationale. Hasidism succeeded in creating communities of mystics of the mundane world, with the Hasidic leader replacing the mystical master and teacher.

The selections from the writings of the Jewish mystics down the ages, which are included here under the title "Stories and Sayings," all belong to what we have called the human face of the Kabbalah. There is little straight theosophy and what there is, is devoid of complex symbolism. Since the vast majority of all kabbalistic works are theosophical or technical (though when the complexities of the teachings they contain are explained at length they often have something striking to say), it was impossible to use them as material. Instead we have drawn on tales about the mystics, on some of their sayings scattered throughout kabbalistic and nonkabbalistic texts, and primarily on the writings of some of the great Hasidic mystics who produced a new genre of mystical literature aimed at the layman. The wisdom of the Hasidic mystics is of special interest and relevance to modern man since the Hasidic masters seem to speak in a contemporary idiom.

In making the selection, an effort has been made to include as much material as possible that is not available to the reader who knows no Hebrew. Certain of the Hasidic teachers have been allocated more space than others, since apart from considerations of balance or availability, an attempt has been made to present teachings that are likely to speak directly to the soul of the reader. If someone gains some knowledge of what this or that school of mysticism was trying to say, well and good; if he also gains some insight into his own life and that of the world around him all the better. The Jewish mystics themselves never saw their task as one of providing information; life was too short and man's tasks too urgent to spend much time collecting facts. No doubt a striking Hasidic story may go down well at a cocktail party, but the Hasidic masters always emphasized the existential dimension of their teaching. A man should not say "How cute" or "How clever," he should always ask himself whether what he has heard or studied has affected his service of God in any way. They were willing to borrow songs from the peasants to teach their Hasidism if they felt that the lilting melody of an anonymous shepherd could help bring their own flock one iota nearer to God. No doubt the academic student of Jewish mysticism will be annoyed time and again by the lack of respect for names and dates among the Jewish mystics. Had they known that their works would be studied and analyzed, dated and located, at some future time by meticulous scholars it is still unlikely that they would have dotted their "i's" and crossed their "t's." If they sometimes did not put their name to a work, that was not out of any disrespect for the reader but out of a desire that the text itself should be studied for what it contained, not for who wrote it.

Part 2
Stories and Sayings

THE FOLLOWING IS a prayer, ascribed to R. Moses Cordovero, which should be said before the study of Kabbalah.

"Who sits on high but whose providence directs the worlds below. God of all emanated worlds, one and unique, master of awe and true judge, emanator of all emanations, creator of all creatures, former of all that has form, source of all action. Who is able to conceive of one myriad part of the great loftiness of Your wondrous deeds, let alone of the forms which You have formed. Who could think of knowing even one myriad part of the hidden secrets which are inherent in Your creation, let alone any infinitesimal fraction of Your emanation, with which the one and unique master unites himself in complete union.

"Therefore Father of Mercy forgive and pardon all my sins and transgressions. For all my organs and sinews, and the dimensions of my soul are like sheep without a shepherd. We have desecrated things which we cannot rectify without the great flow of divine light which comes from the heights above through the channels of divine light. Therefore may it be Your will, Lord my God and God of my fathers that You should purify my soul in all dimensions, that I may be fit and worthy to awaken the Lower Waters through the study of holy mystical texts. Remove the covers from my eyes that I may behold wonders from Your Torah. Make me worthy to be illumined by the light of Your Torah in order to understand the beauty of the secrets of her mysteries. . . . May the beauty of the - our God be on us and the work of our hands established for us. May the words of my mouth and the meditations of my heart be in accordance with Your will, God my Rock and Redeemer."

II

Once four Talmudic sages went on the mystical journey to Paradise. They were Ben Azai, Ben Zoma, Aher (the name by which Elisha ben Avuyah was known), and R. Akiva. R. Akiva said to them: When you reach the stones of pure marble be careful not to say "Water, water," for it is written "He who speaks falsehood cannot stand before my eyes." Ben Azai gazed and died; Ben Zoma gazed and went mad; Aher cut the plants (i.e. became a heretic); R. Akiva came out in peace.

III

R. Akiva used to teach his pupils that they should accustom themselves to say: All that the Merciful One does is for the good. It once happened that R. Akiva was on a journey and coming to a town at dusk he tried to find a place to lodge but without any success. He said: All that the Merciful One does is for the good, and went off to spend the night in the fields. Now he had with him a cockerel, an ass, and a lantern. During the night a wind came and put out his lantern, a cat came and ate up his cockerel, and a wild animal came and devoured his ass. On discovering this he said: All that the Merciful One does is for the good. On returning to the town in the morning he found that it had been sacked by a band of roving soldiers during the night. He said to his pupils afterwards: Did I not tell you that everything which the Holy One does is entirely for the good? [If the lantern had stayed alight, the ass had brayed, or the cockerel had crowed, then the soldiers might have come over to where R. Akiva was to investigate, and slain him too.]

IV

R. Akiva used to say that it is better to make one's Sabbath into an ordinary weekday rather than to become dependent on the charity of others.

V

Once the Roman authorities made a decree that Jews were not allowed to study Torah (i.e. the Bible and its interpretation). R. Akiva ignored the decree and carried on with his regular lectures. Pappos ben Judah passed by and found R. Akiva expounding Torah in public. He said to him: Akiva, are you not afraid of the Roman authorities? R. Akiva replied: Let me tell you a parable. A fox was walking along the bank of a river and saw the fishes swimming around wildly in groups from place to place. He asked them what they were running away from, to which they replied that they were running away from the nets that the fishermen used to trap them. He said to them: Perhaps you would like to come up on the riverbank, and we will dwell together in harmony. The fishes answered him: Is it really you who is called the wisest among the beasts? You are not wise but a fool. If we are afraid in a place which is our element and which gives us life how much more so in a place which means death for us. So it is with us, for the Torah is our element.

VI

When Moses went up to Heaven to receive the Bible he found the Holy One sitting and filling in little crowns over the letters of the Torah. Moses said to Him: Master of the Universe, why is it necessary to add these crowns? God replied: At the end of several generations there will be a certain man called Akiva ben Joseph who will interpret each little extra decoration and learn many precepts from them. Moses said to Him: Master of the Universe, show him to me. Move backwards, said God. Moses went and sat at the back of R. Akiva's class. He could not understand what they were being taught and his spirit sank. When they reached a certain issue R. Akiva's pupils asked him: Rabbi how do we know this? To which R. Akiva replied: This is a tradition which goes back to Moses at Sinai. On hearing this, Moses's spirit revived.

VII

After Elisha ben Avuyah, otherwise known as Aher, became a heretic, R. Meir his disciple continued to study with him. When people asked in amazement how R. Meir could learn Torah from the mouth of the heretic Aher, he replied that he ate the fruit of the date and threw away the inedible peel.

VIII

When Elisha ben Avuyah was buried, fire came down from heaven and began to burn his grave. Some people came and said to R. Meir: Your master's grave is being consumed by fire. R. Meir rushed out and spread his cloak over the burning grave: If God does not want to save you then I shall have to save you, he said.

IX

Ben Zoma used to say: How much trouble Adam, the first man, had to go to until he obtained bread to eat. He had to plough, to sow, to reap, to bind the sheaves, to thresh, to winnow, to grind, to sift, to knead, and to bake. Only then could he eat. Whereas when I get up in the morning I find all these things done for me.

X

Ben Zoma would try to make people see things in a new light. He would say: Who is really wise? He who learns from everyman. Who is really mighty? He who conquers his own evil inclination. Who is really rich? He who rejoices in his own portion. Who is really honored? He who honors his fellow man.

XI

Ben Azai said that those who do not have children are like unto those who shed blood and diminish the image of God in the world. Whereupon the rabbis said to him that some people preach well and practice well, others practice well but do not preach well, but Ben Azai the bachelor preaches well but does not practice what he preaches. What can I do? Ben Azai replied. My soul is in love with the Torah. The world will have to be populated by others.

XII

Ben Azai said: The reward of a good deed is a good deed. Whereas the reward of an evil deed is an evil deed.

XIII

The Zohar tells how R. Simeon bar Yohai fled to the wilderness of Lod together with his son Eleazar, and they hid in a cave. A miracle occurred and they were provided with a carob tree and a spring of water. They ate the carob fruit and drank the water. The prophet Elijah used to come to visit them twice a day, and to teach them. And nobody knew they were there.

XIV

R. Simeon bar Yohai says in the Zohar: Woe to those people who maintain that the Torah only comes to show us stories and everyday matters. If this were so, even in our day we could create a Scripture of these ordinary matters, and a better one at that. If Scripture were there to tell us historical events, then in the court records of the kings of this world there are finer things. So one is forced to say that the words of the Torah are of a high level of spirituality and contain profound mysteries. The stories of Scripture are the garments in which the real Torah is clothed. It is like a man's garments which everybody sees. Fools think that when they have seen a man's clothes they have seen the real man and do not need to look any further. They take the clothing to be the body of the man. There are those who think when they have seen the body itself that they are acquainted with a man's soul. So it is with the Torah. It has a body which is made up out of the commandments of Scripture; this body is clothed in clothes which are mundane stories. Fools of this world only look at the clothes, which are the stories of the Torah, and they know nothing more, nor do they look at what is underneath these clothes. Those who are better informed do not look at the clothes but at the body which is under the clothes. The wise ones (i.e. mystics), servants of the Supreme King, who have stood at Mount Sinai, only look at the soul of the Torah, which is the essence of everything, the real Torah.

XV

The Talmud tells how R. Johanan said to R. Eliezer: Come. I will instruct you in the mysteries of the divine vision. I am not yet mature enough, R. Eliezer replied. By the time he was mature enough R. Johanan had died. R. Asi (a pupil of R. Johanan) said to R. Eliezer: Come and I will instruct you in the mysteries of the divine vision. Had I been worthy of them, R. Eliezer answered, I would have learnt them from R. Johanan your teacher.

XVI

The Midrash teaches: God looked into the Torah and created the world.

XVII

The Midrash teaches: Why is God called by the name Makom meaning "place"or "space"? Because he is the space of the world, but the world is not his place.

XVIII

The Tosefta warns: Many teach about the mystical vision of God without ever having seen it themselves.

XIX

The Zohar teaches: And God said: Let the earth bring forth a living spirit according to its kind. All the spirits of the world are made up from male and female components. When they leave the heavenly world, they leave as male and female, and then their paths split up. If a man is worthy these two elements will later on be reunited, that is, he will find his soul mate.

XX

The Zohar teaches: At the time when the Holy One created the world and wanted to reveal deep matters from their hidden recesses, and light from within darkness, they were intertwined with one another. Because of this, that out of darkness came light and from out of the hidden recesses were revealed deep matters, that one came from the other, it also is the other way round: out of the good emerges evil, and out of love emerges strict justice, since they are intertwined.

XXI

The Zohar teaches: The Holy One said to the created world: Let us make man, I and you. I will make the soul and you will provide the body! So it is that the body comes from the three levels of physical reality . . . and the soul is given by God. . . . That is why the soul is separated from the physical mundane world and longs and desires for higher levels of holy spirituality . . . and that is why it is of eternal duration.

XXII

The Zohar teaches: When the Holy One created the world he made all the creatures of the world, each according to his form, and afterwards he created man in the spiritual form of the higher world, and gave him control over everything through this form. As long as man stands in the world all the creatures of the world bow their head and look upon the high spiritual form of man, then they are all in awe of him. . . . But this is only true when they can see this form, the soul within him.

XXIII

R. Judah the Pietist tells the following story in his Sefer Hasidim: There once was an illiterate cowherd who did not know how to pray, so instead he would say to God: Master of the Universe, you know that if you had cows and you gave them to me to look after I would do it for nothing, even though I take wages from everyone else. I would do it for you for nothing because I love you. A certain sage chanced upon the cowherd and heard him praying in this manner. The sage said to him, You fool, you must not pray like that. The cowherd asked him how he should pray, and the sage set about teaching him the order of prayers as they are found in the prayer book. After the sage went away the cowherd soon forgot what he had been taught and so he did not pray at all. He was afraid to say his usual prayer about God's cows because the sage had told him that it was wrong to say such things; on the other hand he could not say what the sage had told him because it was all jumbled up in his mind. That night the sage was reprimanded in a dream and told that unless the cowherd returned to his spontaneous prayer great harm would befall the sage, for he had stolen something very precious away from God. On awakening the sage hurried back to the cowherd and asked him what he was praying. The cowherd told him that he was not praying anything since he had forgotten the prayers the sage had taught him, and he had been forbidden to tell God how he would look after his cows for nothing. The sage begged him to forget what he had told him and to go back to his real prayers that he had said before ever he had met him.

XXIV

The Spanish mystic R. Moses ben Nahman taught: The thoughts of the Patriarchs (Abraham, Isaac, and Jacob) were not separated even for one moment from the divine light. Through all their physical activities the whole focus of their mind was directed towards God. Even during the time when they associated with their wives in sexual union their thoughts were not separated from cleaving to the divine.

XXV

R. Moses ben Nahman said: A person should keep God and His love in his consciousness at all times. He should not separate his thoughts from Him when he journeys on the way, nor when he lies down, nor when he rises up. Until he reaches the spiritual level at which when he speaks to people he speaks only with his mouth and tongue, but his consciousness is not with them—it is in the presence of God. It is possible for those who reach this spiritual level that while they are yet alive they are bound up in the bond of eternal life. For they themselves have become a dwelling place for God's divine Presence.

XXVI

One day, a Friday, the Ari went out with his colleagues, as was his custom, to welcome the onset of the Sabbath in the fields outside Safed. He said to his associates: Let us now go to Jerusalem, and let us rebuild the Temple, for I see that this moment is the End of Days leading to Redemption. Some of those present said: How can we go to Jerusalem at just this moment seeing that it is many miles away? Others of his circle said: It is good, and we are ready to go. But first let us return and tell our wives so that they will not worry about us, and then we shall go. Then the Ari cried out with tears welling up in his eyes, and said to the members of his association: I call heaven and earth to bear witness that from the time of R. Simeon bar Yohai to this moment there was no more fitting hour for redemption than now. If you had agreed to this then the Temple would have been rebuilt and the scattered ones of Israel gathered in to Jerusalem. But now the moment has passed, and Israel has reentered exile anew.

XXVII

The holy Ari said to Rabbi Moses Alshekh (who desired very much to study Kabbalah) that his soul had not come into the world for this, and that in a previous incarnation his soul had already learnt sufficient theosophic wisdom. But R. Moses was very insistent so the Ari said to him: I will give you a sign. Tomorrow, go to the place which I and my circle of mystics always pass by on our way to welcome the Sabbath. If you see us going along the road, know that I am only trying to test your perseverance. But if you do not see us know for sure that your soul did not come into this world to study kabbalistic wisdom. When R. Moses heard this it seemed to him a very good idea, so around midday on Friday he put on his Sabbath clothes and sat by the roadside to wait for the Ari and his colleagues to pass. He remained waiting patiently for their coming, but just when the moment arrived he fell into a deep sleep. The Ari and his circle went by, and he did not see them. When the Ari's party was returning, he told his disciples to awaken him, because the sun had already set. R. Moses stood up in utter confusion: What have I done? All day I was waiting and looking, and just at the crucial moment I fell asleep.

XXVIII

Once when the Master, the holy Ari, was sitting in the House of study with his disciples he looked at one of them and said to him, Go out from here, for today you are excommunicated from heaven. The disciple fell at the feet of the Master and said to him, What is my sin; I will repent for it. So the Master said to him: It is because of the chickens you have at home. You have not fed them for two days, and they cry out to God in their hunger. God will forgive you on condition you see to it that before you leave for prayers in the morning you give food to your chickens. For they are dumb animals and they cannot ask for their food.

XXIX

Once the Master, the holy Ari, passed a large synagogue in Tiberias. He showed the disciples a stone built into the wall, and said: In this stone is incarnated a soul which asks me to pray for it.

XXX

Once a high official of the local government came to visit R. Jonathan Eybeshutz. When he entered the rabbi's study the latter stood up to greet him, and they stood there talking a considerable time. Eventually the official said in a somewhat puzzled tone of voice: Why does the rabbi not invite me to sit down in his house? To which R. Jonathan replied: From the moment you entered my house it became your house and you became the master here. Therefore it is not for me to ask you to sit down. Quite the contrary.

XXXI

Although heavenly powers wanted to give Elijah, the Gaon of Vilna, mystical and theosophical secrets through the medium of daemons, who were masters of secret knowledge and princes of the Torah, without the necessity of human effort, he refused them. He said that on numerous occasions heavenly mentors came to him volunteering to hand over to him the mystical secrets of the Torah without any effort on his part and he refused to take any notice of them. He said: I do not want what I acquire of God's holy teaching (Torah) to come to me through any intermediary of whatever kind. Instead I am completely dependent on God and what he wants to reveal to me of his Torah, through my own labor which I am engaged in with all my might. He will give me wisdom, and an understanding heart. In that way I shall know that I have found favor in His eyes.

XXXII

Elijah, the Gaon of Vilna, said that what the soul attains, the wonderful and awesome levels that it reaches, in the state of sleep, through the upward journey of the soul to higher worlds, is not the main thing. What is important is what a man achieves while incarnated in this world in the waking state through his own struggle and effort. It is then that man can exercise his free choice and clear his mind of all else but concentration on spiritual matters.

XXXIII

For more than fifty years, Elijah, the Gaon of Vilna, never slept more than half an hour at any one time during the night, nor did all the periods of his sleep total more than two hours. Even when he was weak and sick he never forsook his sacred studies. He would get up during the night in great awe, wash his hands, say the morning blessings with indescribable joy and love, and then stand on his feet from before midnight till dawn, a period of more than eight hours, studying with a voice both melodious and awesome. The sound of his voice burnt with a spiritual fire so that anyone who heard it was struck by soul-stirring feelings of holiness.

XXXIV

There was in the city of Vilna a certain man, a dreamer of dreams, whose awesome dreams astounded everyone who heard them. Through them this man was able to tell people what their conversations and deeds in their private rooms were. He was brought before the Gaon Elijah, and the dreamer said to him: Two weeks ago, on a Thursday, you sat in this very room and expounded mystical teachings; to your right sat R. Simeon bar Yohai and to your left the Ari. The Gaon was astounded as to how a human being could know this. He then looked carefully into the face of the dreamer and it dawned on him that this man was a manic depressive, and the dreams of a manic-depressive are occasionally true and full of insight.

XXXV

Elijah, the Gaon of Vilna, once asked his friend the Maggid of Dubno to give him ethical instruction so that he might strengthen himself in the service of God. Now the Gaon was known as a man of saintly disposition who spent all his waking time secluded in his room in study, prayer, and contemplation. So the Maggid of Dubno said to him: It is easy to be a gaon (sage) and a saint cloistered here in your room. You should go out into the market place and try to be a saint there.

XXXVI

R. Haim of Volozhin taught: In truth all the secrets and mysteries of the Torah are really perfectly explicit and revealed, it is only that our eyes are covered and we do not see. The same is true of nonmystical matters in the Torah. Sometimes a man can put great effort into trying to understand a small and simple thing. After he understands he is amazed that he should have had such trouble with the idea when it is quite obvious. The fact is that man is often struck by blindness. If a man involves himself in the study of the Torah without any thought of self, God will open his eyes and remove the mask of blindness.

XXXVII

R. Haim explained the text which states that one of the miracles which took place in the Temple was that when the worshippers stood together in the court-yard they were terribly crowded, yet when they bowed down during the Temple service there was always enough room for their prostrations, as follows: When they stood upright and proud and full of their own ego—they were crowded for space. But when they bowed down and humbled themselves before God— they had plenty of room.

XXXVIII

R. Haim taught: This is the way of man. No man of Israel should say in his heart, What am I, and what power do I have to do anything in the universe with my ineffectual actions? Rather he should understand and know and fix amongst the thoughts of his heart that all the details of his deeds, words, and thoughts, at every moment of time, are not lost. For every one of them rises to its root to produce effects at higher spiritual levels. In truth when a man understands this fully, his heart will tremble within him.

XXXIX

R. Haim taught: The very source and root of the Torah in the upper, hidden spiritual worlds is really far above these worlds themselves. It lies in the beginning and source of the divine emanatory process from the Godhead. But it has come down onto earth, as it were, to illumine the world with its glory. God has handed it over and planted it in our midst so that we can hold fast to the mystical Tree of Life. The vitality and very existence of the various spiritual worlds thus depends on man's involvement with and contemplation of the Torah. If we meditate on the Torah and hold fast to it, then we cause the source of the Torah in the upper worlds, the wellspring of holiness and blessing, to pour forth blessing, eternal life, and an awesome holiness on all the spiritual worlds, each world according to its level of holiness and ability to receive the divine flow.

XL

According to the Hasidic tradition: The essential root principle of the Hasidic teaching of the Besht is that a man should always remember that he has a duty to serve God at every moment, whether at the time that he is studying Torah, or praying, or performing some mundane physical activity, or occupied with worldly matters, or just having an ordinary conversation. Before him is always an element of good and an element of bad, and he needs to isolate the bad aspect and reject it, while isolating and strengthening the good element. In this way he serves God always, and it is as if he was engaged in the continual study of Torah even though he is walking about the market place.

XLI

The Besht said: Sometimes the Zaddik (Hasidic Master) sits amongst people and speaks with them about mundane matters, or tells stories, and seems to be wasting his time. But in truth he is cleaving to God totally in thought, and so what he says, even though it seems to concern trivial matters, is a vehicle for spirituality and holiness.

XLII

According to the Besht the Messiah will plead even on behalf of the wicked, claiming that they are really righteous. Because of this they too will repent and so they too will be saved. A minor Zaddik loves little sinners, a great Zaddik loves great sinners as well, but the Messiah will love and plead for even the utterly wicked. Everyone who emphasizes the good in all creatures has within him an aspect of the Messiah.

XLIII

The Besht taught that in all of a man's sufferings, be they physical or spiritual, one should think that God himself is also to be found in them, only they are a clothing for him. When one realizes this, the clothing is removed and the suffering disappears.

XLIV

Everything in this world, the Besht explained, has within it holy sparks, even trees and stones. These sparks are even contained in all that a man does, even in his sins. When he repents for his sins he raises these sparks back to their source in higher spiritual levels.

XLV

The vitalizing soul of man, said the Besht, is one aspect of the vitalizing source of all living and created being, namely of the Holy One himself, as it were. When a man meditates on the thought that he is rooted in the divine, and he prays to God, then he performs an act of true unification.

XLVI

Someone once asked the Besht why it was that sometimes when a man cleaves to the Creator in the very middle of his cleaving he finds himself suddenly very distant from God. The Besht answered him with a parable: When a father wants to teach his son to walk what does he do. He takes his son and stands him on the ground in front of him, puts his hands out on either side so that the child does not fall, and the child walks between his father's hands. When the child comes close to where his father is standing, the father withdraws a little so that the child will come on further and further. Thus the child learns how to walk. So it is with God. When a man burns with religious fervor and cleaves to God, he withdraws from him, so that a man learns how to strengthen himself more and more in his cleaving to the divine.

XLVII

The Besht taught that a man should believe with perfect faith that his deeds, words, and every movement of his, everything is God himself. For it is he who controls man and limits his divine presence within him. Realizing this, a man will not seek any kind of reward for his deeds since it is God himself who is the doer, and not man.

XLVIII

When a person tastes something, the Besht taught, he should perceive with his understanding that the good within food and drink is nothing other than God himself, from whom all pleasures derive.

XLIX

The Besht said: If a man accepts everything that happens to him in this world with love, then he will have both this physical world and also the higher world of the soul.

L

The Besht taught that a man should contemplate that there is nothing in the whole universe except God himself, who fills the whole world with his glory. The essential part of this contemplation is that a man should think of himself as absolutely nothing, for he is really only the soul within him, which is a part of the divine itself. Thus the whole of reality is only the one God himself.

LI

The Besht taught that God's hiddenness behind the world, and the mystic's journey towards him, can be understood by the following parable: There was a king who created through his magical art, barriers and walls, one within the other, with which to surround himself. All these were, however, really illusory. He commanded that money be spread around at the gates of each of these walls to see how great the determination and desire of his subjects, how much effort each one of them would make, to come to the king. There were those of his subjects who immediately returned home after they had collected a little money at the gates of these illusory walls. There were others who got as far as the second or third walls. But there were very few who did not desire to collect merely physical treasures only to reach the king himself. After considerable effort they came to the king and saw that there were really no barriers and walls, everything was a magical illusion. So it is with God. Those who truly understand know that all the barriers and walls of iron, all the garments and coverings are really only God himself in hiding, as it were, because there is no place where he is not.

LII

The Besht taught: It is known that the Evil Urge in man always dresses itself up in the guise of a good deed. If it were to tell man to sin straightforwardly, man would not listen to it. So it has to dress itself up; but inside is the Evil Urge itself.

LIII

When he heard of the great reputation of the holy Rabbi Israel Baal Shem Tov, and how everyone was journeying to him, Rabbi Dov Baer of Mezeritch, who was a scholar of considerable erudition, decided to visit him and test him. He wanted to know whether the Besht was really at such a high level or simply a charlatan. When he came to the Besht he thought he would at least hear some scholarly teaching, instead the Besht told him some stories. The same thing happened on the second day of his visit. The stories actually contained a wonderfully profound message, but R. Dov Baer did not understand. Disappointed he returned to his inn and prepared to return home. As he was about to leave the Besht sent for him. Do you know how to explain kabbalistic teachings? the Besht asked him. Yes, he replied. So the former showed a certain passage in a mystical text to R. Dov Baer, who contemplated it for a few moments and then explained it to the Besht. I am afraid you really do not know anything, said the Besht. R. Dov Baer looked at the passage again and said to the Besht: That is the correct interpretation; if you know a better way of explaining it please tell me. The Besht started explaining the passage and as he did so the whole room was filled with light and a burning flame surrounded him, and they both saw that the angelic forces mentioned in the passage were present. Your interpretation was the correct one, the Besht said, but your way of studying lacked soul.

LIV

Once on the festival of the Rejoicing of the Torah, the Besht's disciples were making merry and dancing, and were drinking a lot of wine from the Besht's cellar. The Besht's pious wife said to him: Tell them to stop drinking and dancing, otherwise you will not have any wine left for sacramental purposes. The Besht said to her with a smile, You tell them that they should stop and go home. When she opened the door they were dancing in a circle, and she saw that they were surrounded by a burning flame, like a canopy of fire. She herself took the jugs and went down to the cellar to bring them as much wine as they wanted.

LV

Once one of the Besht's pupils wrote down the teachings he had heard from him. The Besht had a vision in which he saw a demon walking around holding a

book in his hand. He said to him: What book is that
in your hand? The demon replied: This is the book
that you have written. Then the Besht understood that
someone was writing down his teachings. So he gathered all his disciples together and asked them who had
been writing down his teachings. The disciple who was
responsible admitted that he had done so, and brought
him his writings. The Besht looked through them and
said: There is not even one word of mine here.

LVI

The Besht said that anyone who tells stories about
the greatness of the Hasidic Masters, it is as if he were
engaged in the deepest mystical doctrines (Maaseh
Merkabah).

LVII

It is told of the Besht that he once crossed a river without using any kabbalistic incantation, but simply by
stretching his belt over the water and walking across
through the power of great faith alone.

LVIII

The Besht followed the way of the Ari, namely to
reveal God's divinity in this lowly world. Everything
that the Ari revealed was, however, on a cosmic level

involving very elevated spiritual dimensions which not every consciousness is capable of grasping. But the Besht revealed God's divinity here on earth, especially in the ordinary man no part of whom is anything except a garment for the divine power which is hidden within him. The same is true of all mundane matters since there is no place empty of God.

LIX

The Besht wrote in one of his letters: Once I performed the mystical exercise of the elevation of the soul into the upper worlds, and I saw wonderful things in a vision, things the like of which I had never seen before and which are impossible to relate even in personal conversation. When I returned to the lower Paradise I saw souls of the living and the dead moving from world to world by means of the mystical path in great joy and they asked me to go with them. So I requested my heavenly mentor to accompany me because of the great danger of rising into such high spiritual worlds. I entered the hall of the Messiah and asked him: When are you coming, Master? He answered: The sign of my coming will be when your teachings will be publicized and revealed in the world.

LX

R. Ephraim, the grandson of the Besht, told the following parable: Once there was a man who could play a musical instrument with great skill and sweetness. All those who heard him play were unable to resist the music, and they broke into dance with spontaneous joy. A deaf man chanced by and he could only see people jumping around and he thought they were demented. He asked himself: What manner of joy is this? In truth if this deaf man could experience the great pleasure and sweetness of the music he too would join the dance.

LXI

The Maggid R. Dov Baer taught: Every lock has a key which fits it exactly, according to the shape of the lock so is the shape of the key. But there are thieves who are able to open the lock without a key by breaking it open. So for every hidden mystical matter there is a key, namely the mystical state of consciousness directed at that matter. But the real key is to be like a thief who breaks through all locks, and the way this is done is by breaking one's own ego, in great humility. In this way the barrier which locks man in, and divides him from the dimension of the divine, is broken down.

LXII

A man must separate himself from all attachment to the physical reality, said the Maggid, until he rises through all the spiritual worlds and becomes one with God, his own individual existence having been annihilated. Then he is really called man.

LXIII

The Maggid R. Dov Baer taught: "The creation of heaven and earth was the bringing forth of something from nothing, but the work of the Hasidic Masters is to bring out the mystical Nothing from this something."

LXIV

Dov Baer, the Maggid of Mezeritch, said to his disciple the holy Rabbi Zusya of Hanipoli that in the service of God he should learn three things from a child and seven things from a thief. From a child he should learn:

1. always to be happy;
2. never to sit idle;
3. to cry for everything one wants.

From a thief he should learn:

1. to work at night;
2. if one cannot gain what one wants in one night to try again the next night;

3. to love one's coworkers just as thieves love each other;

4. to be willing to risk one's life even for a little thing;

5. not to attach too much value to things, even though one has risked one's life for them, just as a thief will resell a stolen article at a fraction of its real value;

6. to withstand all kinds of beatings and tortures but to remain what you are;

7. to believe that your work is worthwhile, and not to be willing to change it.

LXV

The Maggid taught: The splendor of God cannot be borne by any of the worlds. So God contracted his splendor through a number of contractions in order for it to be borne because He wanted to rejoice in the work of his hands. This can be understood from the parable of a father who has a small son. The small son wants to take a stick to ride on pretending it's a horse, even though the horse should lead the man and he wants to lead the horse, nevertheless he gets fun out of it. So his father helps him and gives him a stick to satisfy him. Thus the righteous want to lead the world, so God created worlds in order that they should have joy with them. For the Glory of God's essence is totally beyond our grasp, but we can appreciate his Glory as it is manifested in the different worlds. Therefore he contracts himself into these worlds in order to rejoice in the joy which the righteous have in these worlds.

LXVI

R. Schneur Zalman used to sing: God I do not want your Garden of Eden, and I do not want your Paradise. I want only you.

LXVII

When R. Schneur Zalman of Liadi's first book on Hasidic mysticism appeared, R. Levi Isaac of Berdichev said of it: This book, the Tanya, is amazing. Such a great and mighty God put into such a small book.

LXVIII

When R. Schneur Zalman of Liadi was in prison (on trumped-up charges) he was visited by a government official who was impressed by the rabbi's saintly appearance. The official, who was an educated man and well acquainted with the Bible, asked the rabbi if he would mind answering a question that was bothering him, and the rabbi agreed. Please explain to me, said the official, what it means when it says in the Bible that God called Adam and asked him: Where are you? How could God not have known where

Adam was? The Rabbi replied: Do you believe that the Scriptures are of eternal validity, and they exist for each age, each generation and each man? Yes, said the official. The rabbi continued, The verse in Genesis where God calls Adam means that in every age God calls to each man and says to him, Where are you? Where are you in the world?

LXIX

R. Schneur Zalman taught: Everyone who has insight into the matter will understand clearly that everything created and having being is as absolute naught with regard to the Activating Force, which is in all created being. This Force constitutes its reality and draws it forth from absolute nothingness to being. The fact that all created things seem to have existence and being in their own right is because we can neither conceive nor see, with our physical eyes, the Force of God which is in the created world. Were the eye able to see and conceive the vitality and spirituality in each created thing, which flows through it from its divine source, then the physicality, materiality, and substantiality of the created world would not be seen at all; because apart from the spiritual dimension it is absolute nothingness. There is really nothing in existence besides God.

LXX

R. Schneur Zalman taught: It is clear and understood by everyone that there is a great difference between the spiritual attainments of the mystics, like R. Simeon bar Yohai or R. Isaac Luria, which are the attainments of intuitive knowledge and wisdom, and the attainments of the prophets through prophecy. For in the spiritual attainments of the mystics the hidden God does not reveal himself as a manifestation (as is the case with the prophets), but they achieve the esoteric wisdom of the hidden itself.

LXXI

The essential purpose of knowledge, said R. Schneur Zalman, is not that people should know the greatness of God from authors and from books. The essence is to deepen one's awareness of God's greatness, and fix one's thoughts on God with the strength and power of the heart and mind. Thus one's thoughts will be bound up with God, with a strong and powerful bond, as it is bound up with the physical things that one sees with one's own eyes.

LXXII

Once during the morning when R. Schneur Zalman of Liadi was sitting drinking coffee, holding his glass in his hands, he talked about the holiness of his colleague R.

Zusya. Master of the Universe, he said: Why is it that
the Zaddik R. Zusya when he thinks about the divinity of even a small part of the universe, the awe of God
falls on him, and his bowels give way from the great fear
he feels, whereas I, who understand all the kabbalistic
mysteries of the cosmos, nevertheless remain steady
and do not tremble? As he was speaking a great shaking
and trembling overtook him, and the glass fell from his
hand, his face started burning like fire, his eyes bulging;
all this went on for about half an hour.

LXXIII

Once, R. Dov Baer of Lubavitch, the son of R. Schneur Zalman, was learning in his house and beside
him was his daughter in a cradle. The child fell to the
ground and lay there crying bitterly, but because of
his deep concentration R. Dov Baer heard nothing.
His father, R. Schneur Zalman, who was learning in
an attic room, came down, picked the child up, and
put it back in its cradle. It's amazing to me, he said to
his son, that your mind is so constricted. When you
are involved with something there is no room in your
mind for anything else. I am not like that. When I am
involved in deep contemplation I can still hear the
noise of the fly crawling up the windowpane.

LXXIV

The Hasidic master R. Kalonymous of Krakow taught that the value of going to visit a truly saintly teacher can be understood thus: A man may imagine that he has reached a high level in his service of God. But when he goes to visit a truly saintly master he realizes that all his deeds to date are without worth, for he can appreciate the high level of the master's service of God. Thus a man can turn to God in truth and repent.

LXXV

It is reported that R. Zusya never taught Torah to his disciples around the Sabbath table, as was the general custom. The reason for this was that the pupils of the Maggid only used to teach what they had heard from their master around the Sabbath table, and this R. Zusya could not do. For when the Maggid used to begin to teach he would open with a verse from Scripture which began with the words: And God said, or, And God spoke. When R. Zusya heard these words from the mouth of the Maggid he would immediately feel a mystical illumination, and start moving to and fro. This caused a disturbance so they had to take him outside. He would stand in an outer room and climb up the walls shouting: And God said, or, And God spoke, in a loud voice. Only when the Maggid had finished his discourse would R. Zusya calm down.

LXXVI

Rabbi Zusya said: I would like to be able not to eat, but what can I do since my Creator simply forces me to by the fact that he has created a mouth for me. Now surely God did not create anything in his world except to serve him alone, therefore why did he need to create a mouth to eat and such like, except that one can serve him with one's mouth. In everything in this world there is a spiritual essence which needs to be raised to God.

LXXVII

It is told of R. Zusya that all his service of God was with great awe and soul cleaving to the divine, accompanied by an annihilation of his physical existence. Many times when his soul flew up to cleave to God he would abandon his this-worldly existence until he nearly ceased to exist, and would have to force himself to remain incarnated in his body.

LXXVIII

Once R. Zusya prayed that he should be able to achieve the great awe of God which the angels have. He acquired such a tremendous sense of fear and awe that he was unable to stand or sit for even one moment. He hid himself, now under the bed, now in the dark corners of the house, and was unable to bear the great awe so that he almost died. He prayed to God that he should be a man once again. He said afterwards that man in his physical form is unable to attain this level.

LXXIX

Once when R. Zusya was going around collecting money for the redemption of Jews taken captive, he came to an inn and saw a bird in a birdcage. Here I am dragging my feet around collecting money for captives, he said, but surely there is no greater redemption of captives than letting this bird go free. So he opened the cage and the bird flew off. When the landlord returned and found out what had happened he went up to R. Zusya and said: You madman, how could you do such a terrible thing. Do you know how much money it cost me? And he beat R. Zusya cruelly. R. Zusya said to him: I am going around to collect money to ransom people in need; you too will find yourself in need some day. Many years later the ex-landlord, now a poor man, came begging at R. Zusya's door and told him how all his possessions had been destroyed in a fire and he was left with nothing.

LXXX

When R. Levi Isaac of Berditchev heard that a seventy-year-old Jew in the neighborhood had become an apostate and left the Jewish fold his immediate reaction was to say: You see, O Lord, the spark of holiness which resides within your people Israel. It took this man's evil inclination seventy years before it could entice him into apostasy.

LXXXI

On one of the major Jewish fast days R. Levi Isaac passed by the house of a Jew and found the owner sitting in his doorway and eating publicly. The rabbi reminded the Jew that the day was a fast day, but the Jew assured him that he was well aware of the fact. Then surely you must be unwell and eating under doctor's orders, said the rabbi. Not at all, replied the Jew, I am perfectly healthy. At this point R. Levi Isaac gazed up to heaven and addressed God: Master of the Universe, see how this Jew is attached to the truth. He is unwilling to excuse himself if this means uttering a falsehood.

LXXXII

R. Levi Isaac of Berditchev being a Hasidic Master had many opponents in the town where he served as rabbi, since it was a stronghold of the anti-Hasidic party. Once his opponents took the opportunity of his absence from the town to kidnap his wife and children, and to send them out of town on a wagon full of manure. The followers of R. Levi Isaac were incensed at this barbarous act and they hurried off early next morning to the

Hasidic rabbi of the neighboring town. They told him the story just before he went off to the synagogue for his morning prayers, and they were convinced that he would seek out justice from God who would punish these evildoers. When the Hasidic rabbi returned from his prayers he had to admit to the Hasidim of R. Levi Isaac that his prayers for justice had been of no avail, for R. Levi Isaac himself as soon as he had heard of the incident had prayed to God for forgiveness for those of the anti-Hasidic party who had perpetrated the act.

LXXXIII

Once towards the close of the Day of Atonement, when Jews fast and pray for twenty-five hours, R. Lev. Isaac of Berditchev felt that through his prayers he had almost succeeded in bringing about the Messiah. So he began to put a last great effort into his prayers in order to complete the task. Suddenly he became aware that there was a Jew in the synagogue, very faint from fasting, and that if he, R. Levi Isaac, delayed the conclusion of the prayers any longer the man would die. So R. Levi Isaac quickly concluded the synagogue service and declared the fast at an end. The effort to bring about the coming of the Messiah had to be abandoned.

LXXXIV

When the Hasidic leader R. Shmelke came to Nikolsburg to accept the appointment as rabbi of the town,
all the townsfolk came out to greet him. He asked
them to allow him an hour to himself before the official reception, and he was shown into a private room.
One of the more inquisitive townspeople wanted to
find out what the new rabbi would be doing by himself during this hour so he hid close to the door and lis-
tened in to what was going on. To his utter surprise he
heard the rabbi saying over and over to himself "How
do you do rabbi of Nikolsburg, how do you do learned
rabbi and teacher" and such like greetings. When R.
Shmelke left his private room at the end of the hour the
man could not refrain from asking him what the point
of his remarks was. The rabbi replied: I was afraid that
when the people greeted me at the reception I would
feel pride at the respect they were showing me. So I
addressed myself over and over with those same titles
of honor until I realized how ridiculous they all were.

LXXXV

Once a preacher came to the town of R. Meir of Premyslan and preached a long and powerful sermon in
the synagogue. Before departing he went to visit R.
Meir to say goodbye and found the rabbi's house full
of townspeople who had come to bring the rabbi gifts
of silver and gold. Why is it, thought the preacher to

himself, that I gave such a wonderful sermon yesterday, and nobody has offered me any money, while to this rabbi they give so freely? The rabbi immediately sensed what was passing through the preacher's mind, so he said: It is known that a spiritual leader influences his flock, and passes on his personality traits to those whom he teaches. Now I despise money and all that I receive I give away to those in need. Those who come under my influence also learn to despise money and they bring it to me. You, however, love money and you cause those to whom you preach to love it as well. Hence they do not give it away.

LXXXVI

R. Nahman of Bratslav made it his habit to continually begin anew in his service of God. When he fell from the spiritual level he had attained, he did not feel depressed because of this. He merely said that he would begin anew as if he had not yet begun to enter the service of God, and that only now was he beginning for the first time. Sometimes he would have to begin again several times in one day, because even in the course of one day he might fall several times from the intensity of his service of God.

LXXXVII

R. Nahman said that no one has attained true humility unless he is on a level where he can say to himself that he is humble.

LXXXVIII

R. Nahman was strongly opposed to those who maintained that the high level of spirituality of the Hasidic Master was due to the fact that he had been given a very lofty soul. He said this was not true and the essential point lay in the good deeds, effort, and activity of the man himself. He explicitly stated that every man in the world is capable of attaining a very high spiritual level; this only depends on man's choice, and on nothing else.

LXXXIX

Sometimes his pupils would hear R. Nahman say explicitly: How does one become worthy of being a Jew? He would say this sincerely and with great simplicity as if he had not yet entered the spiritual life. This was how it always was. He would continually move from level to level even though he had already attained great and awesome levels of spirituality. Nevertheless he was never satisfied with this. He would say on many occasions: Now I know nothing at all, absolutely nothing. About himself he would say that his teachings were unique, but his ignorance was even more unique.

XC

R. Nahman would say that if he knew that he was now on the same spiritual level as yesterday, he would not want to be himself at all.

XCI

R. Nahman would say that the true goal of knowledge is the realization that one does not know. In each branch of knowledge this idea is operative, therefore even though one achieves such a realization in one area of knowledge this is not yet the final goal. One needs to strive to achieve a higher realization of ignorance at higher levels, ad infinitum.

XCII

It is very good to cast yourself in total reliance on God, and to depend on Him. My way is as follows, said R. Nahman, as each day begins I give over all my movements to God, in order that they should be according to His will, then I have no worries about whether things are turning out right or not, since I rely upon Him.

XCIII

R. Nahman would go to great lengths to emphasize the wonderful nature of God. He said the greatness of God was without measure, and that marvelous things were done in the world all the time, but they are so awesome that we simply have no conception of them.

XCIV

A truly religious man finds it very difficult to be rich, said R. Nahman, and even though there are some righteous people who have wealth it is very difficult for them and detrimental to their service of God.

XCV

R. Nahman taught: The Evil Inclination in man is like someone who runs amongst people with his hand closed, and nobody knows what is in it. He tricks people and asks each one: What am I holding? And each person assumes that the closed hand holds something he desires very much. So everyone runs after him. Eventually he opens his hand and there is nothing there at all.

XCVI

R. Nahman taught: All worldly desires are like beams of light which enter a house from the sun's rays. They seem to the senses to be solid, but when someone tries to take hold of such a sunbeam there is nothing in his hand at all. Just so are the desires of this world.

XCVII

You should know that a person can shout very loudly (to God) in the silence of one's inner still, small, voice, said R. Nahman, and no one will hear him because no sound leaves him. Thus a man can stand amongst a number of people and cry out loudly, yet nobody can hear him.

XCVIII

R. Nahman taught: When a man is continually in a state of joy then he can easily set aside an hour during the day to talk to God with a broken heart, and to pour out his soul before Him. But when a man is sad and depressed it is difficult for him to isolate himself with God, and to speak openly to Him. Therefore a man has to make an effort to be joyous always.

XCIX

R. Nahman taught: Through depression and sadness a man can forget who he really is. Therefore it is necessary to be continually in a state of joy, no matter what low level a person may be at. Through joy also, one can give renewed life to another. For there are people who suffer greatly and they walk around full of suffering and worry. When someone approaches them with a happy face he is able to give them renewed life. To do this is not some empty matter but an exceedingly great thing.

C

R. Nahman taught: A man needs to have faith in himself believing that he is beloved in the eyes of God. For the greater God's goodness the more valuable man is in his eyes. Feeling unimportant and distant from God is not humility, and a person should always ask God to be worthy of true humility.

CI

R. Nahman taught: Since the whole earth is full of God's Glory, a man must nullify his own personal traits until he nullifies himself completely before God. The more he nullifies himself the more the light of God is revealed to him. For when one places a physical object in front of light a shadow is produced. The greater the object the greater the shadow, and the shadow masks and hides the light.

CII

Once when R. Nahman was walking outside the city in a grassy field he said to his companions: If only you were worthy to hear the sound of the songs and praises of the grass. How each blade of grass sings to God, without any egoistical motive and without any thought or expectation of reward. How beautiful it is to hear their song, and how good to serve God in their midst, in awe.

CIII

R. Nahman said: Why should one worry about his livelihood? There is nothing really to worry about except that one may die of hunger if he has no livelihood. And so what if he dies. For he must die anyway.

CIV

R. Nahman said to his followers that it is not true, as is generally assumed, that stories help people fall asleep. In fact stories help people who sleep away their lives to wake up to the deeper realities of existence. He said to them: I will soon begin to tell stories. Among the mystical fairy stories which he told are the following: Once a king said to his good friend the Vizier that he had looked into the astrological constellations and foreseen that all the wheat that would grow in the coming year would make anyone who ate of it mad. So now we have to put our heads together and devise a plan. The Vizier suggested that the best thing to do would be to set aside some wheat now, from last year's harvest so that they, at least, would not need to eat of the diseased wheat crop. But the king answered: If so, then we alone will not be mad, for it is impossible to set aside enough wheat now for everyone, and the rest of the world will be mad. If we are the only sane ones in a mad world then it will really be we who are mad. There is only one alternative. We too will have to eat of the wheat, but let us make a sign on our foreheads to indicate to us that we are mad. When we look upon each other's forehead we shall see the sign and know that we are mad.

CV

R. Nahman told the story of how a king's son became mad. He imagined that he was a turkey, and that he had to sit naked under the table and scratch around amongst the pieces of old bones and breadcrumbs. All the doctors in the realm despaired of being able to help him or cure him, and the king was frantic. Eventually a wise man came and said that he would undertake to cure him. He too stripped himself naked, sat under the table next to the king's son, and began to scratch among the breadcrumbs and the bone meal. The king's son asked him who he was and what he was doing there. The wise man replied: And what are you doing here? I am a turkey, he said. I, too, am a turkey, said the wise man. So they sat together for some time until they became used to one another. Then the wise man indicated that some shirts should be thrown to him, and he said to the king's son: Do you assume that a turkey cannot wear a shirt? He most certainly can wear a shirt and still remain a turkey. So they both put on shirts. A little later the wise man indicated that they should throw him some trousers, and as before he said: Do you think that just because someone is wearing trousers he cannot be a turkey? So they both put on trousers. It went on like this until they were both fully dressed. The wise man then indicated that they should throw them down some human food from the table, and he said to the king's son: Do you think that just because one eats good food one cannot be a turkey? One most certainly can. So they both ate together. After that he said to him: Do you think that a turkey has to be under the table? It is possible to be a turkey and to sit at the table itself. In this way the wise man continued until he had completely healed him.

CVI

R. Nahman told how a certain man from a certain town saw in a dream that in the city of Vienna under the bridge a treasure was buried. He journeyed to Vienna and stood by the bridge trying to figure out how to go about uncovering the treasure, since it was impossible simply to dig it up in the daytime because of the number of people about. A soldier passed by and said to him: What are you doing, standing here lost in thought? The man said to himself that it was best to tell the soldier the whole story because he might be able to help him, and they could then split the treasure between them. When the soldier heard the tale he said: You foolish Jew, fancy taking notice of a simple dream. Why I myself have dreamt that in a certain town in the house of a certain man, under the wood store there is a treasure. Do you think that

I would journey there to look for dream treasure? So the man returned home and dug under his wood store, and sure enough he found the treasure. He said: Now I know that the treasure is always with you, but to find out about it you have to journey far away. So it is with one's spiritual life, R. Nahman concluded. Each one possesses the treasure himself, but to find out about the treasure he must journey to a spiritual guide.

CVII

R. Nahman told the following story: Once a poor man who made a living by digging up clay which he used to sell, found a precious stone in the clay. On having it valued by an expert he was told that the stone was too expensive for anyone in his country to buy, and that he must go to London and sell it there. The poor man, not having much money, sold all he had and went collecting money from door to door till he had enough to journey to the nearest seaport. There he wanted to board a ship, but he had no money to buy a passage so he went to the captain and showed him the diamond. The captain said: You must surely be a great man, and he immediately took him on board ship with a show of honor. He was given a first class cabin with all the accompanying luxuries. During the voyage he would take out the diamond from time to time to look at, particularly at meal times when he sat alone dining in his cabin. Once he sat down to his meal and placed the diamond on the table so that he could feast his eyes on it, and having eaten a good meal he fell asleep. The steward came in as he slept and removed the tablecloth with the crumbs on it, which he shook out into the sea. When the man awoke and realized what had happened he nearly went out of his mind. What could he do? The captain was a blackguard who would think nothing of killing him if he found he did not even have the cost of the passage. He decided that the only thing to do was to pretend that nothing had happened and to put on a happy and relaxed front. When the captain next came to visit him in his cabin he smiled and was happy and the captain noticed no difference in him. The captain said to him, out of the blue: I know that you are a straightforward and wise man, and I would like you to help me. You see I'd like to buy grain at one of our ports of call and resell it in London at great profit. Because I am the captain of the ship I am not supposed to do any business transactions so I would like to register the deal in your name. Naturally I will pay you for helping me out. The passenger agreed to the captain's proposition, and the captain acquired the merchandise. When the ship docked at the port of London the captain died of a sudden stroke and the passenger was left with a fortune in merchandise, worth much more than the diamond would have fetched. When R. Nahman finished the story he said: The diamond was not really his, and the proof is that he lost it. The grain was his, and the proof is that it remained with him. The reason why the poor man came into his own was precisely because he held on (by keeping up an appearance of joy and not giving in to despair).

CVIII

R. Nahman taught: Just a little coin when held up in front of the eyes can prevent one from seeing a great mountain, even though the mountain is thousands of times bigger than the small coin. So this little world prevents man from seeing the great light of the Torah, because the world stands in front of one's eyes and masks his sight. But just as it is easy to remove the coin from before one's eyes, and one immediately sees the great mountain, so by simply removing this world from one's eyes, one is able to perceive the great light of the Torah.

CIX

R. Nahman of Bratslav taught: You should know that in life a man has to pass over a very, very narrow bridge, but the essential thing, the most essential thing, is that he should not be afraid—at all.

CX

R. Nahman told the following parable. The man of true love is a very great man indeed, and the very existence of time depends on him. For there is a mountain and on this mountain is a stone from which a spring flows. Now everything has a heart, including the world itself whose heart is a fully developed structure with face, hands, and feet, etc. But the toenail of the foot of the heart of the world has more heart to it than the heart of any other being. The mountain on which the stone and the spring stand is at one end of the world and the heart of the world is at the other end. The heart longs with an overpowering longing to come to the spring, and cries out because of this longing. The spring too wants the heart. The heart has two weaknesses. The first is that the sun pursues it and burns it because it wants to draw near to the spring. The second weakness is the great and overpowering desire which it has to come to the spring, standing as it does on the opposite side of the world. When the heart needs to relax a little in order to regain its strength then a great bird comes and spreads its wings over it, and protects it from the sun's rays. Why then does the heart not go to the spring if it longs for it so much? The reason is that if it wants to go towards the mountain it cannot see the top of the mountain and so loses sight of the spring, and not being able to see the spring it would die. If the heart should perish then so would the world, for it gives life to everything. So it cannot move but stays where it is with its overpowering longing. The spring has no time, for it is not within time at all. The only time which the spring does have is what is given to it as a present by the heart. This present consists only of one day and were this day to draw to a close then the spring would have no time and would disappear. If this happened the heart too would be unable to continue to exist without its beloved spring, and if the heart died so would the world. So when this day is drawing to a close the man of true love gives one day as a present to the heart, and the heart gives this day to the spring, so that the spring has time once again.

CXI

R. Nahman taught: You should know that even sins and evil things receive their vitality from God, and this is true also of unclean places and houses of idolatry—they too need to receive their vitality from him. But they receive from the hidden divine word, at the level of generality, and the Glory of God within the hidden divine word is utterly, and totally, concealed. For they are unable to receive their vitality from God's Glory and the divine words as they are revealed in the world.

CXII

R. Nahman taught: A person should know that God's Glory fills the whole earth, and there is no place empty of him. For he fills all worlds and surrounds all worlds, and even a person who is engaged in business dealings with heathens cannot excuse himself and say: It is impossible to serve God because of the grossness and coarseness which I meet all the time. For a man can find aspects of the divinity in all physical matters and in the language of the heathen as well. Without this divinity they would have no vitality and existence at all, but this divinity is greatly contracted and present in just sufficient an amount to give vitality, and no more. The lower the level of emanation, the greater the contraction, the more the divine light is clothed in many garments.

CXIII

R. Nahman taught: It is known that the Sitra Ahra (literally "Other Side," i.e. evil) surrounds holiness. In particular a person who is drawn after sin is drawn after the Sitra Ahra, his place is there and the evil surrounds him on all sides. When his spirit revives and he wants to repent, he finds it very difficult to pray and to speak to God; his words and prayers are unable to pierce the barriers and screens which surround him and to rise up. They linger on his side of the barrier. When, however, he repents truly then his illuminated words split through the barriers and they take with them all his previous efforts at speech and prayer which have remained behind until now. How does one become worthy of being able to do this? The main thing is truthfulness, for everything depends on truth, and one must follow the truth according to the level that one is on. As the rabbis teach: The seal of God is truth.

CXIV

R. Nahman taught: When God wanted to create the world there was no space to create it, for everything was Ein Sof, the Unlimited. Therefore he withdrew his light to the sides and through this contraction a vacant space was left. In this space the creation of the world took place, and this vacant space is necessary for the very existence of the world, for without it there could be no place for the creation. Now there is a certain form of heresy, a wisdom which is no wisdom, which concerns deep matters which cannot be grasped and so it seems like wisdom. This heresy involves problems and questions, which really contain no wisdom and are entirely invalid, but because the human mind cannot answer them seem to be wise questions. In truth, however, it is impossible to resolve these heretical problems and questions because they come from the vacant space in which, as it were, there is no divinity. It is impossible in any way to answer these questions, that is to find God in this empty space. If one could find God there then it would not be empty, and everything would just be Ein Sof, the Unlimited.

CXV

R. Nahman taught: The Torah is a garden, and the souls of Israel are the grass and the herbs which grow in the garden. From where do they sustain their growth? From the well which is Wisdom. And how do they receive this Wisdom? Through prayer.

CXVI

R. Nahman taught: Just as when people are happy and dance, they snatch up those who are standing at the side feeling in low spirits and depressed, and force them into the whirl of the dance, so it is with joy itself. For when a man rejoices then depression and suffering stand at the side. A person should try and chase after his depression and force it into the rejoicing, so that the depression itself is turned into joy.

CXVII

One of the things that R. Nahman emphasized to his disciples was that they should not simply study his teachings but they should turn them into prayers. One such prayer runs as follows: May it be Your will, O

Lord our God and God of our fathers, that you abolish wars and bloodshed from the world, and draw down a great and wonderful peace on the world. Let all the dwellers on earth recognize the truth for what it is, namely that we have not come into this world for the sake of strife and conflict, Heaven forbid, nor for hate, jealousy, provocation, or bloodshed, Heaven forbid, but we have come into this world in order to recognize You and know You.

CXVIII

When R. Abraham Isaac Kook was asked why he loved those who were known to be sinners and anti-religious, he replied: It is surely better to err on the side of causeless love than on the side of causeless hatred.

CXIX

R. Abraham Isaac Kook taught that the truly righteous do not complain about wickedness, instead they increase righteousness; they do not complain against unbelief and heresy, instead they increase faith; they do not complain about foolishness, instead they add wisdom.

CXX

Once when Rabbi Kook was walking in the fields, lost deep in thought, the young student with him inadvertently plucked a leaf off a branch. R. Kook was visibly shaken by this act and turning to his companion he said gently: Believe me when I tell you that I never simply pluck a leaf or a blade of grass or any living thing unless I have to. Every part of the vegetable world is singing a song and breathing forth a secret of the divine mystery of the creation. The words of R. Kook penetrated deeply into the mind of the young student. For the first time he understood what it means to show compassion to all creatures.

CXXI

R. Kook lived for many years in the Holy Land, acting for much of that time as the Chief Rabbi of the European Jewish community. He was respected even in non-religious circles for the love and consideration which he showed to all. Some of his more zealous co-religionists, however, were perturbed by the fact that he befriended the secularist and anti-religious farmers and members of left-wing kibbutzim, or collective farms. These zealous Jews saw the secularists as people who were profaning the sanctity of the holy soil of Israel, and they could not understand how R. Kook could acquiesce in their activities. In defense of his attitude R. Kook answered that in the period when there was a Temple in Jerusalem, the innermost part of the Temple, the Holy of Holies, could only be entered by the High Priest. Even the latter could only do so once a year on the most solemn Day of Atonement. Yet while the Temple was being built the ordinary builders and masons were allowed to do their work in all parts of the Temple area, including the Holy of Holies. They were not considered to be profaning its sanctity.

CXXII

R. Kook taught that the true holy wisdom of the Jewish mystical teaching, when it is revealed in the world, vitalizes everything. It is not hostile to any form of knowledge, or to any elevated ideas. On the contrary it crowns them all with a yearning for righteousness, goodness, and humility. The desire for righteousness in all its aspects finds its true source in this holy knowledge. Through this wisdom the desire for righteousness finds its realization in action and in life.

CXXIII

R. Kook warned those who were inclined towards the life of the spirit to take extra care. For the spiritual contemplation of elevated matters may draw a man away from a clear perception of this-worldly considerations. This is one of the defects at the base of prophecy.

Because of it darkness clouds those who attain spiritual heights, and this enables the wicked people of this world, to whom holy ideas are totally alien, to control the world. Thus the glory of holiness is turned into sorrow. Every wise man, therefore, should try to prevent this happening and should use spiritual insight and understanding to increase the clarity of his perception of the world in which he lives, in all its aspects.

CXXIV

R. Kook emphasized the need for each person to develop his, or her, own individuality. He said that it was not the purpose of the many external influences, be they holy or profane, to silence a man's spirit and eliminate his own personal way of seeing things. Their purpose is to pour over him an abundance of lights which he may take into his innermost self, and through them his own insight grows and increases.

CXXV

R. Kook asked why it is that we do not understand the great spirit of life which fills all existence, all creation? Why do we not elevate our ideas to contemplate this great bright light with its infinity of riches and beauty? Why do we not perceive that despite its greatness and power this light is reflected by the limitations and contradictions of our world? We should also appreciate that the holy and awesome source of this light, in the totality of its glorious perfection, is infinitely beyond the spirit of life as it manifests itself in the worlds of our experience.

CXXVI

R. Kook taught that we begin to absorb traces of holiness little by little. One point of light after another flashes on us, like falling drops of rain. These heaven-sent elements as they gather together within us become a great flaming torch. They concentrate their foundation within our souls, and the paths they carve pierce through to the essence of our being.

CXXVII

R. Kook taught that every idea, whether it be from the Jewish teaching or from the world in general, is like a veil hiding the elevated light of a mystery behind the half-grasped idea. This hidden mystery can only be reached through clear inner perception and contemplation of the idea. It is because of this that there is an explicit duty to increase one's knowledge of the holy teachings through continual study. There are exceptional cases, however, when a crack appears in the wall of the cave which normally blocks out the light from above. Through this crack the hidden light suddenly shines, in a way very different from the gradual process of acquiring knowledge. Such miraculous happenings should be received in joy, but one must not rely on the miraculous. The usual procedure should be a movement from the open and revealed to the hidden mystery which underlies them. In such a way one moves from an understanding of the details of existence to a grasp of the totality.

CXXVIII

R. Kook always stressed the importance of the profane and mundane things of this world as a basis of the holy. Holiness has to be built on the foundation of the mundane, for it is the material base to which holiness is the form. The firmer the material base the more important the form which it can bear. Sometimes the holy treats the mundane in a harsh manner, so that the material base is depleted. A period inevitably follows in which the material world reclaims this maltreatment from the holy, and unholy arrogance increases in the world. In the end, however, the holy will subdue the profane not through arrogance but by the absorption of the profane within the holy. For the power of holiness is so much more strong and elevated than that of the mundane.

Index

W

wisdom 3–5, 25, 30, 32, 34, 40, 42, 61, 76, 77, 79, 84–86, 88–89

worlds
  lower 2
  upper 2, 8, 22, 36, 42, 46, 55

Z

Zaddik 47, 48, 62

Zalman, R. Schneur 16, 17, 59, 60, 61, 62

Zevi, Shabbetai 13, 14, 16, 22

Zohar, the 2, 6, 7, 11, 12, 16, 33, 34, 36, 37

Zusya, R. 17, 57, 61–65